CHRISTMAS
WREATHS

THE CHRISTMAS TREASURY

CHRISTMAS WREATHS

NELSON REGENCY
A Division of Thomas Nelson, Inc.

A THOMAS NELSON BOOK

First published in 1993 by
Thomas Nelson Publishers, Nashville, Tennessee.
Copyright © 1993 by
Michael Friedman Publishing Group, Inc.

10 9 8 7 6 5 4 3 2 1

Library of Congress Cataloguing in Publication Data is available.
Library of Congress Card
92-084145
ISBN 0-8407-6916-4

THE CHRISTMAS TREASURY:
CHRISTMAS WREATHS
was prepared and produced by
Michael Friedman Publishing Group, Inc.
15 West 26th Street, New York, N.Y. 10010

Editor: Kelly Matthews
Art Director: Jeff Batzli
Designer: Robert W. Kosturko
Photography Editor: Daniella Jo Nilva
Printed in Hong Kong and bound in China

METRIC CONVERSION CHART

For your convenience, we suggest that you use the following table for adapting to metric measurement. The table gives approximate, rather than exact, conversions.

TO ADAPT LENGTHS

one inch = 2.5 centimeters
one foot = 30 centimeters
one yard = .9 meters

TO ADAPT WEIGHTS

one ounce = 28 grams
one pound = .45 kilograms

CONTENTS

INTRODUCTION

THE CHRISTMAS HOLIDAY SEASON PRESENTS MANY unique opportunities for decorating both inside and outside your home. To reflect the joy of the season and to make your surroundings particularly festive and beautiful, try decorating your home with wreaths—they always make perfect embellishments for the holiday home. Wreaths provide wonderful decoration for the outside of the house—whether they are hanging on a door, in windows, on the porch, or on the garage or barn—providing touches of color and nature to the bare winter landscape. Inside, wreaths bring in warmth and cheer, whether they are hung above a mantel, tucked into a bookcase, or placed on a table as a centerpiece. And wreaths make excellent gifts, allowing you to give a friend or relative a present that was handmade, tailored specifically for them.

An evergreen wreath is one of the most wonderful traditional Christmas decorations. Evergreen wreaths can be purchased from nurseries and florists' shops in a wide variety of sizes. If necessary, their density can be enhanced by inserting short sprigs of holly and boxwood into the branches. It is also very easy to create your own evergreen wreaths from boughs that have either been purchased or gathered from the woods. Balsam is always a favorite, loved for its pungent fragrance, rich color, short needles, and long-lasting freshness. Other greens, such as white pine or cedar, can also be used. (For instructions on creating an evergreen wreath, see page 14.)

A basic evergreen wreath can be embellished in an infinite variety of ways, from a simple design of pinecones, berries, and a generous red bow to an elaborate design including dried and fresh flowers, herbs, fruits, brass bells or horns, or peppermint candies. The choices are endless, limited only by your imagination. And Christmas wreaths do not have to be made of evergreens. This book shows you how you can use both traditional and nontraditional materials to create lovely holiday wreaths with interesting colors and textures.

WREATH BASES

Before you can master the art of wreath making, you must have a working knowledge of the basic wreath forms: straw, wire, foam, and grapevines.

❖ **STRAW**: The straw base is probably the easiest base to work with. It is durable, easy to handle, and porous. Straw wreaths come in a variety of sizes and shapes, the most popular of which are the circle and the heart. Straw bases can hold medium-weight ornamentation or ornaments on florists' picks.

❖ **WIRE**: The wire base is a very widely used frame. Wire bases come in two styles: the crinkle frame and the multiwire frame. These sturdy frames are perfect for making fresh garden wreaths, evergreen wreaths, and wreaths that contain heavy materials.

❖ **FOAM**: The foam base is a very easy base to use; however, it is much less durable than other types of bases. If you push too many florists' picks into a foam base, it will break apart. Also, every inch of the base must be covered so that the white material does not show through.

❖ **GRAPEVINE:** Grapevine bases are the most beautiful and versatile. They can be filled with materials or left relatively sparse, allowing the beauty of the vines themselves to show through and contribute to the design. Grapevine wreaths can be bought in a variety of sizes from three inches to four feet from a craft supply store or florist. You can also make your own grapevine base. To do so, first gather equal lengths of natural vine. Bend one length of vine into a hoop, overlapping and entwining the ends. Temporarily secure the overlapping ends of the vine with wire. Next, intertwine two or three more vines around this main vine the same way. Continue to add new lengths of vine and weave the loose ends into the main vine until the wreath reaches the desired thickness. Last, remove the wire.

TRADITIONAL
EVERGREEN WREATH

A<small>N EVERGREEN WREATH IS A TRADITIONAL CHRIST</small>-mas decoration, in many places synonymous with the holiday itself. A basic evergreen wreath can be bought premade in a variety of sizes. It is much more enjoyable, however, to make your own using freshly cut greens. A homemade evergreen wreath will last much longer and will provide you with the satisfaction of having created something with your own hands.

To make an evergreen wreath base, start with a wire wreath frame, some medium-gauge green florists' wire, a pair of strong scissors or garden clippers, and a large supply of fresh evergreens cut to a uniform size. The larger the wreath frame, the longer the evergreen pieces can be.

There are two basic methods for attaching the evergreens to the wire frame. One method is to simply wire each sprig to the frame, one at a time. The other method is to tie sprigs into small bundles and then attach them to the wreath frame; many consider this the easiest and most effective method of attaching the greens. First, make several clusters of two or three sprigs each by wiring them together at the base of the stems. An average wreath will use anywhere from thirty to forty clusters.

Once you have a good supply of clusters ready, lay the first cluster along the top of the frame with the stems parallel to the frame and pointing toward the right. Tie the end of your florists' wire to the wire frame and begin wrapping it securely around the stems and the frame. Make two or three wraps, and then add a second cluster on the inside of the frame, again with the stems pointing to the right. Secure the second cluster with two or three wraps. Continue to add clusters of evergreens, working around the wreath in a clockwise motion and alternating from the outside to the inside of the wreath frame. When you have come full circle around the wreath, gently lift the ends of the first bundle and secure the stems of the last bundle underneath. Once the wreath is completely wound, you may have to add a few clusters here and there to fill it out. In order to be able to hang the wreath, you can make a loop of craft wire and attach it to the back.

To finish this evergreen wreath, wire pine cones and red berries and then attach them to the wreath foliage. For a polishing touch, add a bow of green brocade ribbon to the top of the wreath.

JUNIPER WREATH
WITH FRESH TULIPS

THERE IS NOTHING BETTER THAN AN EVERGREEN wreath embellished with the traditional Christmas colors of red and white to bring the holiday spirit into a home. This wreath is composed of fragrant juniper, a beautifully textured evergreen, which was wrapped loosely with a deep green ribbon. Instead of using dried flowers, the wreath is decorated with fresh tulips and a star of Bethlehem, which were first placed in waterpicks before being inserted into the wreath. A light layer of baby's breath was the last element to be added.

Although the fresh flowers on this wreath will last only a few days, they can be removed after wilting, leaving a lovely juniper wreath with tiny white flowers that can be enjoyed for weeks.

EVERGREEN WREATH
WITH STRAWFLOWERS

THIS EVERGREEN WREATH WAS MADE ON A FOAM base. The fresh evergreens were wound onto the base with green waxed twine. Next, dried strawflowers in autumnal colors were inserted directly into the foam. Strawflowers are perhaps the best known of the everlastings. Their colors range from white and yellow to orange and brown to shades of pink and red, all of which look stunning against a background of evergreens. For this wreath, a strand of gold-sprayed grapevine, with clusters of grapes still attached, echoes the wreath's circular shape and gives the composition a sense of movement. Pinecones add a traditional holiday touch to the design.

This wreath would be perfect hung on an outside door. However, the way it is placed here—on a mantel strewn with evergreens, grapevines, pinecones, and fruits in addition to a green candle in a brass holder—makes it look extra special.

TWIG AND EVERGREEN HEART

T HIS BEAUTIFUL WREATH OF BLEACHED TWIGS AND evergreens is actually two wreaths in one. Start with a large wire heart for the evergreen base. Then add small amounts of fresh evergreens a bit at a time and wind them securely with green waxed twine. Next, use a small wire heart frame and carefully wind on the bleached twigs. Add the small gold and red balls and the red berries during the winding process to give the wreath a well integrated look. (If you find that winding so many elements in place at the same time is too difficult, add the balls and berries after the twig wreath is completed.) Finally, wire the two wreaths together at the tops of the two hearts, and add a green ribbon and cluster of Christmas balls to hide the connecting point.

EVERGREEN WREATH
WITH BRASS BELLS

B RASS AND EVERGREENS NATURALLY COMPLEMENT each other. This traditional Douglas fir wreath rings in the holiday cheer with a chain of brass sleigh bells cascading from a cluster of gold balls. Anchoring the whole design is a beautiful gold metallic ribbon and a strand of small gold beads that wraps around the entire wreath. Painted Christmas balls or gold-sprayed pinecones or seed pods could also be added to this design or used as less expensive substitutes.

EVERGREEN WREATH
WITH WOODEN SHAPES

NOT ALL EVERGREEN WREATHS HAVE TO BE adorned with such traditional materials as red berries, pinecones, white flowers, or ribbon. This wreath provides a welcome departure from the norm but still conveys the warmth and spirit of the holiday season.

The brightly painted houses and small animals can be made from precut wooden shapes, which can be purchased through a crafts store. The simpler shapes—the tree, stars, and hearts—can be cut by hand. Hot-glue the wooden shapes onto 6-inch florists' picks and insert them into the evergreen frame. Next, wire candy canes (left in their wrappers) onto florists' picks and place them around the wreath. Baby's breath is a wonderful way to simulate the look of newly fallen snow.

EVERGREEN WREATH
WITH HUNTING HORN

THIS EVERGREEN WREATH IS DECORATED WITH A brass horn, which nicely echoes the circular shape of the wreath base. Apples were wired and tucked into clusters of blue cedar berries and ornamental pineapples to create an interesting cluster at the top of the design. The overall feel of this wreath is one of hospitality, with a touch of festivity provided by the gold-sprayed magnolia leaves and pinecones.

This wreath would be perfect to hang on an outside door, welcoming guests inside during the holiday season. However, it would also provide a nice touch hanging in a den or library, particularly if candles also decorate the room because their light will dance off the brass horn and bounce holiday magic in all directions.

EVERGREEN WREATH
WITH CRAB APPLES
AND POPCORN

C HRISTMAS WREATHS CAN BE LARGE OR SMALL,
simple or complex. This large holiday wreath makes
use of just a few materials but arranges them in a fairly
elaborate design. First, a large wire heart frame was covered with boxwood (huckleberry or any other seasonal
green would also work). Next, crab apples were attached
to florists' picks and then inserted into the greens. The
wire frame and the wrapped greens provided enough sup-
port for the crab apples, so no hot glue or wire was
needed. Next, a garland of popcorn, strung on simple
sewing thread, was wound around the heart and secured
at the top of the wreath. To hide the construction and to
add a festive touch, a red satin ribbon was attached to the
top of the heart.

SILVER KING WREATH

SOMETIMES A PARTICULAR FLOWER OR MATERIAL IS so beautiful and distinctive that it needs no embellishment and looks best when it stands alone. The only designing the wreath maker must do is recognize the beauty of the material and display it to best show it off.

To make this silver king wreath, insert short lengths of the stem directly into a foam base. Then add longer lengths to give the wreath fullness and body. Be sure that the stems are different lengths so the resulting wreath does not look too uniform. Also, keep the design open and loose so that light can play off its surface and highlight the texture of the material.

PINECONE WREATH

T HE BEAUTY OF A PINECONE WREATH COMES FROM the pinecones' marvelous variety of sizes, shapes, and shades of brown, as well as their wonderful texture. Spruce cones are tightly packed and make a tailored, elegant wreath. However, the cones of the white pine can also be used effectively. Here, they are made into flowers: when cut in sections, the centers of the pinecones look like the spreading petals of a flower, with a small tufted center. Additional petals can be glued in place for a fuller flower. The center of a cone is quite tough, so the best way to separate the petals from it is with the tips of garden clippers or wire cutters. The tips of the pinecones were also added to the wreath for decoration.

To make this wreath, first soak approximately 20 to 30 white pine or blue spruce cones for a few minutes until they close. Wearing gloves or using a cloth to protect your hands, push these cones between the upper and lower layers of wire on a double-wire wreath frame. You can either have them all facing out (away from the center of the wreath) or you can alternate them. If they all face out, the outer edge of the wreath will be more solid-looking. If you alternate, you can fill in the spaces with other cones for a less regular effect.

Allow the cones to dry overnight or put the wreath in a slow oven to dry and open. While you are doing this, wire an assortment of other cones and seeds of various sizes. A fine wire cut in lengths of 8 and 12 inches is best. To wire the cones, slip the middle of a piece of wire under the top row of petals (scales) on a cone and pull it tightly. Twist the ends together securely so the wire does not slip. There should be two tails of equal length. By placing the wires under the top line of petals, you can pull the tails toward the stem to attach the cone so it points directly up or leave them extending out to the side for attaching flat.

Beginning with the larger cones, attach them along the center, covering the wires of the wreath frame completely. Push the wire tails through the wreath, and twist them together at the back, securing each cone tightly.

Don't cut these wire tails until you are finished. This allows you to find them again if you decide to rearrange the cones and also gives you spare wire with which to fasten the other cones.

Fill in the spaces with successively smaller cones and seeds, ending with the hemlock cones and other tiny ones to fill in all the spaces where wire or frame shows. These should be glued in place by touching the stem end to the point of a hot-glue gun. It is better to put the glue on the seed and then the seed on the wreath than it is to try to get a dot of hot glue into the right place.

PINECONE HEART

For anyone who lives near coniferous woods, pinecones are a plentiful and free material to work with. They should be gathered before the rains of fall and the snows of early winter have damaged them. It is best to pick pinecones on a dry day that has been preceded by other dry days so they will be open and visible to you.

However, those who live in the city or any other place where pinecones are not available can still make lovely pinecone wreaths. This wreath was made from pinecone rosettes that were purchased from a crafts store. The pinecones already had picks inserted into their crowns, making the process of creating this symmetrical heart wreath very easy. The rosettes were first sorted by size. Then, starting with the smaller ones, they were attached to a straw-heart base in such a way as to form a pattern of textural interest. This method creates a wreath that is just as lovely as the one with hand-picked, wired pinecones on page 34, but it took far less time to make.

MINIATURE
PINECONE WREATH

THIS MINIATURE PINECONE WREATH WAS MADE WITH tiny hemlock cones purchased from potpourri suppliers. To make one yourself, first draw around a dish or can to make a circle on a piece of mat board. Draw around something smaller to make the inside circle. The band of board between the drawn circles should be about ¾ inch to 1 inch wide. Cut along the lines to form a ring.

Working over waxed paper and beginning at the outer edge, glue a row of cones to the edge of the ring, lying them on their sides and pointing outward. Repeat on the inside edge. Then fill in the area between them, covering the cardboard base completely. You can make the center row of cones into tiny cone flowers by snipping or twisting them in half to remove the tips. Use these tips and single petals to fill in any spaces where the base shows. Finally, glue a loop of ribbon to the back of the wreath for hanging.

LIVE PARTRIDGEBERRY WREATH

WREATHS DO NOT NEED TO BE HUNG; THEY CAN make beautiful centerpieces during the holiday season. This lovely wreath is made of partridgeberry, a low-growing forest plant with glossy leaves and bright red berries. If you are gathering your own partridgeberries from the woods, take some moist soil and pine needles home from the forest floor to keep the roots damp until you can get the plants home. Keep the roots moist at all times, storing the partridgeberry in a plastic bag in the refrigerator if you must keep them for any length of time before using them.

To make this wreath, fill a small, double-wire wreath frame with sphagnum moss, and wrap it with thread or fishing line to secure the moss in place. Soak the wreath well by submerging it in water for about half an hour, then lift it out and set it on a round plate with a rim or a shallow, flat-bottomed bowl that is a little larger than the wreath frame. Into this moss base, carefully tuck the tiny roots of the partridgeberry, twining the stems along the top to cover the moss with leaves and berries. Leave the wreath in the plate of water for a few days until the plants have taken root enough to stay in place. Then lift and hang the wreath.

During the day, hang the wreath outdoors, bringing it in at night and returning it to the dish of water.

GOLDEN BRANCH WREATH

THERE IS AN INFINITE NUMBER OF WAYS TO USE metallics on Christmas wreaths. This design is very simple and elegant, and the placement of the cluster of leaves and foliage just off-center keeps it from looking boring or conventional. This project is first formed as a swag, then converted to a wreath.

To form the swag, cut a 54-inch length of medium-gauge wire, and wrap it with floral tape. Beginning at one end and working its full length, tightly bind bunches of very slender tree or bush branches to medium-gauge wire, using fine-gauge wire on a reel. Allow the branches to overlap. To convert the swag to a wreath, bend it into a hoop, overlapping the stems, and bind it securely in place with fine-gauge wire.

Next, spray the entire wreath with gold paint and let it dry. To prepare decorative leaves or foliage, spray them with gold paint and let them dry. Using fine-gauge wire,

wire the gilt leaves or foliage in clusters and set them aside. Last, tie and hot-glue a bow to the front of the wreath and then hot-glue the leaf clusters as you desire.

GILDED WREATH

W HEN CREATING A WREATH, IT IS VERY IMPORTANT to keep in mind that the design should flow rhythmically and still invite the eye to rest here and there. A wreath can be symmetrical if the look you desire is one that is tailored and neat. However, an asymmetrical design is often more interesting for the wreath's circular format.

This gold-dipped wreath is filled with pods, cut palmetto, and sea-grape leaves that were wired onto a grapevine base. The bright metallic gold rings in a festive holiday mood. However, the finishing touches—preserved green magnolia leaves, glittered baby's breath, and a red stain ribbon tied around the design—draw the eye around the wreath and provide focal points, preventing the individual elements from becoming lost in the monochromatic gold scheme.

WHITE SPARKLING WREATH

THERE ARE NO OFFICIAL RULES ABOUT WHAT MATE-
rials can or cannot be used on a wreath. As a
designer, you can choose to work with any material that
appeals to you. Although dried and fresh flowers and
other natural materials make beautiful designs, sometimes
you want to create something that immediately captures
the eye, that sparkles and glitters in a burst of holiday
exuberance.

This wreath was made with a variety of contempo-
rary elements that capture the frosty, wintry feeling of the
holidays. The composition includes small packages
wrapped in metallic-colored papers, glittered white baby's
breath, strands of opalescent beads, white Christmas balls,
small opalescent leaves and stars, and a festive silver ribbon.
Most of the elements were simply hot-glued onto the glit-
ter-treated grapevine branches with a hot-glue gun; a few
of the heavier ornaments needed to be wired in place.

WREATH WITH TIN ORNAMENTS

T HIS WREATH WAS INSPIRED BY A VARIETY OF TIN Mexican ornaments, which were arranged to provide a narration of the Christmas story. The design is united both thematically and tonally: the tin ornaments were toned with ochre acrylic paint to bring out the relief details and to match the hues of the dried yellow roses and calmondin oranges that are also included.

The ornaments were arranged symmetrically on the boxwood base to best tell their story—they were first hot-glued onto florists' picks, the smaller ones on 3-inch picks and the larger ones on 8-inch picks. Note how the two large angels highlight the star at the top, and the church and other elements clustered above it provide a counterbalance at the bottom.

NOSEGAY WREATH

THIS WREATH IS A CLEVER DECORATION FOR A HOLiday party. Both attractive and functional, it is composed of individual nosegays that can be detached from the white-painted grapevine wreath base and given as gifts to guests as they depart for the evening.

The nosegays are composed of sprigs of herbs, dried flowers, and a cinnamon stick, which were first wired together with florists' wire and then covered with gold metallic ribbon and collared with gold doilies. The nosegays were then inserted into the hollow, open spaces of the vine wreath, securely but not so tightly that they can't be removed without too much trouble or awkwardness. Gold balls and long stems of painted pods were also added to the base to make the wreath more visually interesting.

TOY WREATH

No one enjoys the holidays more than children, and this wreath, composed of colored baby blocks, is the perfect decoration to hang in a child's room during the Christmas season.

To construct this wreath, cover the entire surface of a foam wreath base, including the inner and outer edges, with small bunches of baby's breath attached to small wooden picks. Then attach the baby blocks on a proportionately smaller wire ring. Hot-glue the blocks with three lengths of florists' picks, and when dry, insert them into the foam base at angles to the surface of the wreath. The trucks, boats, and cars could be exchanged for little dolls or animals. The final touch is a yellow grosgrain ribbon attached to the top of the composition.

LAUREL LEAF WREATH

FRESH LAUREL IS A WONDERFUL SUBSTITUTE FOR traditional evergreens. It has interesting clusters of leaves, and it looks great alone or used in combination with other greens and natural materials.

This wreath was made by cutting short stems of laurel and poking them into a foam ring, making sure to completely cover it. A few laurel clusters were sprayed a copper color and, after they dried, were placed randomly around the wreath design. As an embellishment, balls covered in ribbon of copper metallic and two shades of blue metallic were also added, contributing weight and giving accent. A copper gauze ribbon bow intentionally placed off-center is the final touch.

VINE WREATH
WITH FOLK DOLLS

NATURAL DARK GRAPEVINES ARE THE PERFECT BACK-ground for a pair of folk dolls, charmingly lit by miniature clear electric lights. The wreath has a rustic, country air, and the addition of light provides a small sense of magic that is perfect for the holiday season.

To make this wreath, position and wire two or three stems of dried hawthorne berries in a swag at the top of a 12-inch grapevine base. Then position and hot-glue the dolls inside the circle. Last, add the lights around the form, concealing the wires by tucking them between the vines.

WILLOW WREATH
WITH BERRY SWAG

T HIS WREATH USES AS ITS BASE A 10-INCH PEELED willow wreath in a twisted rope pattern. It is decorated with a swag composed of two stems of silk berries: one red and one black.

To form the berry swag, intertwine the stems of red and black berries, bending to form a C. Position the swag on the bottom front of the wreath, then tuck in the stems and thread the leaves through the willow vines, securing in place with hot glue. As a final touch, tie a piece of green ribbon into a bow and attach it to the center of the swag.

VINE WREATH
WITH GRAPE CLUSTERS

T HIS BEAUTIFUL WREATH IS SURPRISINGLY SIMPLE TO make. It utilizes just a few elements—three artificial grape clusters, one package of natural and one package of teal eucalyptus leaves, and a Wedgwood-green wired ribbon—that are all allowed to flow freely from the grapevine base. A large part of the woody vine was left unadorned, allowing its natural beauty to harmonize with the other materials and play a part in the design.

This wreath was made by interspersing the natural and painted eucalyptus stems and then poking them between the vines at the top center of the wreath, hot-gluing them in place. The grape clusters were then positioned on the wreath, two on the left, one on the right, and secured in place with fine-gauge wire. Last, a bow was tied and hot-glued at the top.

FRENCH HORN
with EVERGREENS

SOMETIMES IT IS POSSIBLE TO REVERSE THE PRINCIPLES of wreath making to create a new and interesting design. Here, evergreens, which normally form a wreath base, are used as decoration. And a brass horn, which would normally be an embellishment on a wreath, acts as the base itself.

To create this wreath, start with a brass or brasslike French horn, preferably one with a decorative cord and tassel. Next, create an evergreen spray by binding some evergreen branches at their center with fine-gauge wire. Then with some wide ribbon, form a six-loop bow with V-cut streamers, and wire one pinecone and a cluster of berries to each side of the bow.

VINES WITH HOLLY AND APPLES

THIS WREATH IS COMPOSED OF VERY TIGHTLY wrapped grapevines that have been sprayed gold and decorated with gold-sprayed and natural pinecones, strands of holly, and assorted pieces of fruit. The holly can be inserted directly into the vine base and allowed to dance freely around it, but the other heavier elements may need to be wired first in order to stay in place.

The green of the holly, in addition to the deep green of the French ribbon woven through the base, is a beautiful contrast to the gold tones, making the wreath rich without making the composition too heavy. The fruit adds some lighter tones and provides some contrast in texture. A piece of cord tied in a bow adds a final touch of gold.

VINES WITH GINGERBREAD

Gingerbread decorations on a vine base make a perfect ornament for the Christmas season. Make gingerbread according to your favorite recipe and cut out designs freehand or using cookie cutters. When the figures are firm and dry, glue them in place around the wreath.

You can make a bow out of the gingerbread dough by cutting a long strip and forming the two loops, and then make a "knot" with another strip of clay. Set this "bow" on two additional strips to form ribbon tails, and cut the ends in a notched shape.

WREATH with
HOLLY and PEPPERMINT

THIS LOVELY HOLIDAY WREATH IS COMPOSED OF TWO of the most traditional Christmas accouterments— fresh holly and red-and-white peppermint candies— which contrast each other nicely and each form one half of the design.

To make this wreath, begin with a foam base and add a wire loop through which a ribbon could be threaded later for hanging. Then wire small clusters of fresh holly and berries to florists' picks and cover the top half of the wreath with them. Next wire individually wrapped peppermints to florists' picks in groups of two or three, wrapping the wire around the cellophane twists. To mask the line separating the two halves, tie on generous red bows at each side. For variation, you can use any sort of brightly colored, wrapped candy for this design.

BOXWOOD WREATH
WITH PEPPERMINT

THIS PEPPERMINT-CANDY WREATH WAS MADE USING the same method as the wreath found on page 73. But instead of holly, this wreath is composed of boxwood, which is arranged in a striped pattern with the candies. The stripes are separated by metallic ribbon bows.

This wreath makes a perfect festive centerpiece that is also edible. It would look lovely with brass candlesticks placed in the center or with tiny votive candles in glass containers circling the outside.

CINNAMON AND POMANDERS WREATH

A SUCCESSFUL WREATH IS COMPRISED OF MANY ELEments that work together, including texture, contrast, color, and balance. Yet a wreath maker can add an additional, wonderful dimension: smell.

This wreath, made of large pieces of cinnamon that have been hot-glued to a foam base, is an aromatic pleasure to have inside. Clusters of pomander, clove-filled oranges, a lime, and a lemon, each tied with gold cord, are gifts that can be removed, leaving a permanent wreath of cinnamon sticks, pinecones, and silver king. Although this wreath takes quite a bit of time to construct, it is well worth the effort.

BRAIDED BREAD
WREATH

THE KITCHEN IS A WONDERFUL PLACE TO HANG A wreath. A vine wreath with dried herbs woven into it is both attractive and practical, allowing you to pick off the herbs as they are needed during cooking.

This wreath, made out of a dried and hardened loaf of braided Italian bread, is strictly decorative, but it is a perfect ornament to hang in the kitchen during the holiday season. To preserve the loaf, you should coat the top and bottom with a clear acrylic spray. Add greens, small wooden ornaments, and balls by inserting them directly into the bread. A hot-glue gun will ensure that they stay right where you desire. Wire the candy rings to florists' picks and insert these as well.

You can always speed up the drying time by placing your loaf of bread in the oven. Set the temperature on low and leave the bread in until it feels totally hard and dry. Then give it a protective coating.

SMALL CANDLE RING

THE BEAUTY OF THIS WREATH CENTERPIECE COMES from the apples and pears, which have been rolled in sugar so they will sparkle from the light given off by the adjacent candle. To sugar a piece of fruit, coat it lightly with egg white, then with your fingers, sprinkle sugar over its surface. Set the piece of fruit on a wire rack to dry—about 30 to 60 minutes. You can make sugared fruit using white glue, but they will not be quite as translucent.

To create this wreath, start with a straw ring set on a cake stand. Wire sprigs of evergreen and holly onto picks and then insert them into the base. Poke each piece of fruit onto a pick and position them so that the composition is balanced. Finish with a few pinecones and dried roses.

CANDLEHOLDER

THIS CENTERPIECE HAS A FORMAL, ELEGANT LOOK that would make it perfect to use as a decoration for a Christmas dinner party. It is created on a foam ring, which, if moistened, will keep the flowers and evergreens alive until the festivities are over.

Arrange the evergreens, holly, roses, and a few sprigs of eucalyptus berries over the foam ring and then poke them securely into it. The candles also can be inserted into the foam. Some apples and golden pears add a touch of color and whimsy to the design.

DECANTER RINGS

S MALL WREATHS PUT IN UNEXPECTED PLACES CAN make wonderful, whimsical decorations throughout the house. Small wreaths can be hung on a grandfather clock or from a shelf displaying lovely dinnerware.

The wreath on the left was easily constructed from florists' wire and small sprigs of boxwood and fragrant cedar. Two lengths of wire were held together and shaped into a ring to sit loosely over the neck of the decanter. Greenery was added with additional wire, filling the whole circle. Some acorns with stems and leaves that had been sprayed gold and a few hemlock cones were also added. For color, a length of ombré ribbon was wrapped around it and pairs of artificial berries were glued at intervals.

The wreath on the right was constructed from three lengths of gold cording twisted together and secured with wire. Where the pieces were joined, a sprig of aromatic cedar and a cluster of lightly gilded pinecones, acorns, and artificial berries were added.

MINI-WREATHS FOR PACKAGE DECORATION

O FTEN WHEN YOU ARE MAKING WREATHS, YOU ARE left with extra dried flowers or a few extra pinecones. It is a great idea to save these materials and create miniature wreaths that can be used as embellishments on gifts.

The yellow package has a premade cinnamon heart, to which a raffia bow and a few dried strawflowers were added. The mauve wreath is also premade and comes painted; it has been decorated with mauve baby's breath and small flowers from a hydrangea blossom. The wreath below it is made on a small straw base, which has been filled with strawflowers, tiny pinecones, and some baby's breath. The bow is made of cornhusks.

The wreath on the blue package is a foam base that has been covered with potpourri, with a few roses glued to the top. The last gift is wrapped with brown paper and tied with fresh grapevines.

GILDED LEAVES
WREATH

BEAUTIFUL WREATHS DO NOT HAVE TO BE DIFFICULT to make. For this wreath, a loose composition of leaves, pinecones, acorns, and artificial berries were wired to a wire ring that had been wrapped with florists' tape. Everything was then wrapped securely in place with florists' tape. Finally, the entire wreath was given a coating of gold spray paint. The look is rich and lovely, but the time and effort required were minimal.

CHERUB WITH SWEET PEA WREATH

T HIS SIMPLE YET ELEGANT WREATH ADDS A TOUCH of class to any setting. This wreath is composed of three silk sweet pea stems intertwined to form a hoop. The flowers, leaves, and tendrils were arranged to appear as if the entire ensemble was blooming from the cherub's hands. (If you cannot obtain a ceramic angel, any similar figurine will suffice.) A yard or two of green satin ribbon, tied in a bow or other complementary design, can add a festive touch to this elegant wreath.

COUNTRY WREATH

A T HOLIDAY TIME, PARTICULARLY IN CLIMATES WHERE the landscape is bare, outdoor decorations serve as reminders that the holiday season has arrived. This barn is simple and rustic, so it required decoration that was classic and neat. A classic evergreen wreath of pinecones, red berries, red ribbon, and small birds is perfect. It is created on a straw base that was first covered with Spanish moss, and the greens were wired on. Bits of additional greenery to fill in the design as well as the other elements were attached to florists' picks and inserted. This wreath brings a wonderful touch of nature to the holiday season.

WHITE AND LAVENDER WREATH

THE BEAUTY OF THIS WREATH COMES FROM THE variety of the dried flowers used in its construction: bunches of sea lavender, purple Australian honeysuckle, purple statice, and dried rose leaves. Unlike most of the other wreaths in this book, it was first formed as a garland and then converted to a wreath.

First, bind corsages of sea lavender using fine-gauge wire. To make the garland, cut a 32-inch length of medium-gauge wire and wrap it with floral tape; make a loop at one end by bending the wire over and twisting it securely. Insert stems of the first corsage into the loop, binding it in place with fine-gauge wire on a reel. Continue binding corsages to medium-gauge wire, overlapping stems with the next corsage, and working the entire length of wire to form a garland. To convert the garland into a wreath, bend the garland into a hoop, thread the end wire into the loop, bend the straight end